MW01709233

for the beauty
Geysha

all my love

2015

Jeannine

VISIONS

A Book of Poetry

Jeannine Proulx

Spinner Arts Publications, LLC
West Olive, MI

VISIONS

Spinner Arts Publications, LLC
West Olive, MI 49460

ISBN 978-0-9724424-4-2

Dedicated to the open thinkers,
free spirits and beautiful souls
who have enriched my life.

Poetry Pages

Introduction

The first draft of this book was compiled many years ago. It has sat on the shelf in perfect form as I've lived my life throughout those years. Children I love have been born and grown. I've moved, others have moved and through it all, this book has sat patiently waiting to be brought to life, to you.

The poems herein represent memories for me of times long gone by and memories buried too deep to recognize. However, these poems do not live in the past. They have over the years become timeless. They have entered conversations in passing, have been quoted by those who have been privy to read them and have gained a life of their own.

When I went to put VISIONS to publish, I realized it needed a few more poems. Some of these poems I wrote specifically for this book. With them now the whole book feels complete.

May you find the insight, joy and relief I still feel as I read these words, written by another me in another time.

With much love. ~Jeannine
May 2010

VISIONS

The Emperor's New Clothes

He talks of seeing
the separation
shadow style.
The pain, persistent,
life's intermittent joys
marred by that unconditioned
melancholy sadness
that lies beneath it all.
None of us know why,
so how could we know how?
We wake each day,
dress, eat, live, work,
love, play, do.
All with this seeming purpose.
Even the seekers have not
found.
Is it indeed we are the
walking naked?
And no one knows?
Childbirth gives us
momentary pause,
as do sunsets,
earthquakes and tragedies.
But answers?
No. The answers lie buried
too deep
are too numerous and stylized

for any kind of a
collective awakening.
Perhaps that is true karma.
We are here to walk
without cause,
without clue,
making up stories as we go along
to explain
that which has no explanation.
I could never believe those
who say they know
for certain.
'Course then, I've found comfort
once or twice
in being naked.

From Sea to Shining Sea

I cannot see German Osbourne look-alikes
    traveling along wind blown
 piers to sit in window seat
    tables ordering key lime pie,
      dark beer and hot chocolate
where I live.

I do not hear seagulls squawk
    dolphins giggle as herons
bark in protest at the fish boat's
      horn's barrage
where I live.

I have not seen bridges that
    span over acres of hydrogen,
oxygen molecules mixing into a
    whole 'nother atmospheric universe
      yet to be explored
where I live.

But I can see snow, as beautiful
    as any fantasy dream, drifted
      against pines still green.
And I can hear wind and the
    silence that threatens to
anesthetize itself,

as if the absence of children
laughing left a void
of insolence.

And I can see icebergs,
as big as any skyscraper's
awe, living on the moon
Lake Michigan style.

And I can feel comfort,
and calm and serenity
as sweet as any day on any
beach in any land far away
where Pelicans fly.

Beauty

Beauty
lifts the soul
heals the body
calms the mind
feeds the spirit.
Beauty
of life
of death
of all things natural.

Elements,
air. water. land. trees.
Life
is beautiful.
But so is a dead tree branch
floating in the sea.

I fear
what hateful people
hate the most
need the most
lack the most
is beauty.

To cover a woman's face
for greed of
her loveliness

her pricelessness
her power
her beauty.

Why hide a rose?
Because of shame she
is not a butterfly.

We must fight hate
with beauty.

Children understand
crayoned traced hands with
hearts
right where hearts should be
quilted
by hand
with love.

And then shared with those
filled with sadness.

That is beauty.

A hug.
A smile.
A nod.
A touch.

That is beauty.

Plant a tree
        write a poem
lie on the grass
        look up at the sky
and
        soak in rays
                of beauty.

That is how we fight
                                hate.
That is how we fight
                                fear.
That is how we
                defend ourselves
                        against terror.

Share
        the beauty
                that is you.

Do not cower
        under your blankets
                waiting for the terror that
tries to paralyze us all.

Live your life to

the fullest.

Play with your children
inhale the fall air
walk your dog
live your life.

The beauty of you living your life
appreciating every moment
that
can
heal
the
world.

Burst of Inspiration

It was a miscue
pushed the worn button
by accident with an elbow
corrected just as quickly
but we could not
pretend it wasn't there
it didn't happen.
She made a comment
about how the sudden
storm of inspiration for a poem
disappears just as fast
and my mind raced
to a poem written by
Laureate who speaks
of the fleeting idea,
spark, inspiration to be
can be lost in a
moment and how
writing, writing like
photography of thoughts
takes
snapshots of that
moment in time
as I just/ did/
now.

She

So beautiful is she.
Love shining in those kitty cat eyes.
Yet, like the sun
one can see when the clouds roll in
covering her energy,
hiding her smile.
It is in those times she retreats.
Often to sort out the why
behind the smile.
Opening up to others is difficult
when each day she creates a new
alternate reality.
In those times when arms cross her chest
in a desperate embrace
she needs love. She needs reassurance
that the reasons for her joy are real.
That her beauty is not a passing phase
but a sense of her core.
Like the wind gently nudging
the clouds onto another pasture.
She needs someone
wise enough to understand
strong enough to hold secure in her love
a warm body to calm her soul.
For only a smile equal to hers
can beckon those rays
bring back the warmth, chase away the rain.
She will shine again.

Creation

We created time where there was
none before.
We created buildings and windows
and doors.
We created cities to hoard
ourselves in.
We created laughter.
We created sin.
We created a life to enjoy
or bear through.
We created our destinies.
We created we.
So as we complain about this
and of that
we must stop to realize
we created that
too.

Shock

It may feel as though your
heart has shattered
lying pieces on the floor
and all you can do is stare at them
unable to fix what is broken.

It may feel as if life has no meaning,
pointless, obscure.
That all you once believed lies
torn, lying on the floor.

It may feel as though you will
never quite catch your breath again,
sobs being the biggest
gulp of air you can manage
and all you can do is watch the
tears stream out among the wadded up
tissues lying on the floor.

It may feel like that,
as you lay
lying on the floor.

But this is merely the
beginning of a long process
of grieving

of healing
of feeling
of compassionate
being.

And it may take awhile and
it may take more than a few
friends, family, loved ones, time.

But when you are ready,
you will find the strength
to pull yourself up off
the floor
to sit on a chair.

Watching

As I lay on the pink plastic floaty
designed for water use
on my wooden deck with
white plastic chairs
I can look through the bars
protecting me
from the neighbors
and watch the wind
sweep across the pond
and feel the sun's heat
upon my face.
The birds near me
make crunching sounds
as they split the hulls of
sunflower seeds from the feeder
hanging.
They do not know I am listening.
Nor do the ducks know that
I watch
while they preen themselves
upon the sandy bank.
No, only I know I am watching
and that others watch me.
Is that why humans
believe in a god?

In Defiance of Gravity

In defiance of gravity
I sit.
Perched on the seat of my soul
staring at
an endless sunset
that seems to go nowhere
but ends up on the other side
of the world.
I feel like the sun.
calm burning
into waters
so deep I
cannot reach
the bottom.
Stared at by many.
Understood by few.
I melt
into a rainbow
of yesterdays
looking for my
tomorrow.

Nobody Knew

Nobody knows
What the shame felt like.
What the
Secrets felt like.
What the lies felt like.
For me.

Nobody knows
How much time I spent
Wondering when you'd end
Seized up passed out on the floor.

Nobody knows how I laid there
Listening to you breathe
Waiting for that one breath
When you would breathe no more.

Nobody knows
How black I felt.
How grey I lived.
How red I saw.

Nobody knows
The pain I hid.
The days I buried
Deep down in my soul.
Until you opened up

The secret chest
And laid the hidden bare.
In front of trusted friends
And strangers
Most of whom had all been there.

And the tears I cried of memory
Were not just of the pain
But for the miraculous process
That has brought you
Back to me
again.

For You From Me

If there were another
who could make me laugh
but there isn't.

If there were another
who could answer all
my questions
but there isn't.

If there were another
who could handle all
my moods with such grace,
listen to me prattle on and on,
and let me go when I sing songs
and run up to trees and hug them.

But there isn't.

Nobody understands me
like you do
the way you do
how you do
what you do.

Accepting me for me
makes me love you
for who you are

for all you do.

It's what you don't do
to stop me from
being me
that matters most
to me!

Leading by Example

You moved from next door
to behind the door
and I tried to shut you out.
You went from happy and free
to sacred and alone
I tried to let you be.
But the visions of what your life is like
the memories that haunt me so
will not leave me alone in the dead of night
when all my defenses are down.
You are a good friend to me
and to all you see
your life is not so bad.
But, I do know your pain and
the tears that stain pillowcases and
loved ones close by.
I cannot escape
what you mean to me.
I cannot erase your burden.
But I can show you I know
where it is you are at and
what you are feeling has been felt
by someone before.
Someone who learned
to close the door on the world
and open the sky to herself.

BIG

God is too small a word
to describe sunsets,
full moon rises
tides, monkeys and DNA.

God is too small a word
to describe ballet,
Van Gogh and PTA.

God is too small a word
to describe marriage,
money and SEX.

God is too small a word
to describe children,
curiosity and PMS.

God is too small a word
to describe life, love
and common sense.

God is too small a word
to describe the world we live in
full of love, hate and tenderness.

Only Good Girls Go to Heaven

They never told you in kindergarten that
  good can be bad.
They never told you
  set boundaries up front
  even if it makes people mad.
They never told you
  No can mean yes
  to a different question.

In kindergarten I learned to only speak nice.
Bad talking was gossip and
  gossip was evil.
I learned to say Yes
  when someone asked for help
and learned to do onto others
  as you would have done onto you.
I learned to be good
  so I could go to heaven.

I thought I was bad by the time
I left kindergarten.
I like to talk, a lot.
And I said No, too,
  when it was something I didn't want to do.
I wasn't always nice.
I wasn't always fair.
I stole candy from my mother,

quarters from my father
and hid it all in a fort I made upstairs.

High school wasn't much better
in terms of my good girl goal.
Girls who like girls go to hell.
So I knew with the feelings I had
I was doomed for sure.
Men walked all over me.
I just said Yes
like I was supposed to
when anyone asked for help.

I got lost for quite a while.
Mired in feeling bad, but trying to do
what I was told good girls do.
All the while hating saying Yes
to everyone and everything.

It took me six years and four different colleges,
a broken heart and a makeover
to realize while I'd been saying Yes
to everyone else,
I'd been saying No to myself.
I thought that's what good girls did.

I really don't care what good girls do now.
I'm sick of trying to be

because I never was
and never will I be.

I've learned that heaven's the lollipop
the doctor gives you after a shot.
The rabbit in front of the greyhound.
Always so close,
yet somehow out of reach.

Good girls don't go to heaven.
There is no heaven later
and it's hell
we live through now.

Because someone told us in kindergarten
only good girls go to heaven.

Red Bird Sightings

My Red Bird showed himself to me today.
He's been hiding. And I've been avoiding the questions I
must face.

He shows up at awkward moments.
In fleeting thoughts I send through my brain.

I want to believe he listens.
I want to believe he knows.

I know.

I know I've been hiding.
I know I've put off the big questions, the small answers and
the great little big box lies unopened.

I watch for my Red Bird when I want to reassure
that the thoughts I have are honest.
The words I think are clear.

But he shows up at odd moments and causes me
to stare wondering if it was my thoughts
that brought him oh, so near.

Who knows if he answers me

or is just flying on his way.

All I know is the Red Bird stopped and said
Hello to me today.

Clean

I'm craving a cigarette
in the worst way.
A symptom of patterns.
Habits.
Linked together.
Pen and paper.
Smoke and caffeine.
It's harder
not to start again
than
it was to quit.
And somehow I wish
I was sitting in smoking
so as to breathe
second hand
what I crave
and
don't deny
I miss.
My life much cleaner
without anxious. anxiety.
over when. where. how.
A Band-Aid that never healed.
Sealing the dirt in.
I come clean.
And breathe. easy.

To Live, Love and Give as Only You Can

Don't you see?
The world needs more people like you.
calming and strong, loving and kind.
The world needs more people like you.
People who care and
people who share.
Who give to the world
love unconditional.
The world needs more people like you.
Don't you see?
Your purpose in life
is to show others how.
Your actions speak louder
than words ever can.
You have created a
legacy of love that will love on
in every child, woman, man
who ever had the pleasure
of knowing you.
Don't you see?
Can you stand?
The spirit of your love
carries us on,
a beacon of hope
through the murkiest
of times.
You have lead

when others faltered.
loved when all else
failed
And have shown the world
generosity of living,
wisdom of mind, heart of gold
and spirit of soul.
The world needs more people like you.
Don't you know?
Don't you see?
The world needs more people.
Like
you.

Life is a journey. Love is its purpose.
Thank you for being you and doing what you do!

Sweet Soul Mate of Mine

Your lips feel like silk
  on a cool autumn night
when the crickets still chirp
  in the Harvest Moon light.
I could never get enough
  of your kisses.

Your hugs now reborn
  hold me gently tight
as I rest my head
  against your shoulder.
High heels and lipstick.
Your loving looks of wonder
      light my night.
You know me like no other.
Accept me as equal
  and yet allow faults.

My shadow self comical
  once you got to know me.
But you do not tease
  mercilessly.
Never demeaned
  condescending.
You are firm
                but gentle
loving but

stubborn.
How I love
gazing into your eyes.
Sometimes so shocked
by how deep I can see
the real you
the real me
reflected.

We are two halves
to one whole partnership.
Walking side by side
holding each other up.
As together
we walk through this
journey called love.

Generation

A lady smiled at me today and said
You look like an actress
    you won't ever know.
She's far too long before your time.
But you look like her,
  the hair, the smile,
a pixie, yeah, a pixie doll.

I thought of you as she spoke these words,
    a woman that I hold quite near.
I thought of who you might've been
  had you picked up a script and not
a play pen.

I thought of you bending over the sink,
    kids screaming through the halls.
What you thought while lying there
  among the hospital bars.

I thought of what your life was like
    and what it might've been,
an actress, a model, an artist at bay.

You lived like Mother Hubbard.
You looked like Hepburn.

A lady smiled at me today

and in her words I saw
a piece of you not only in her eyes
but in my soul and heart.

And unable to turn away
I looked at her again.
And thought of you
and thought of me
and what we could've been.

Dali

So many things swirling in my head.
pictures and lists, musical art
dancing, a mist flowing.
River time clock.

What day is it?
I forget.
Where do I live?
Who am I?

Too much confusion
other people's problems
I have accepted as my own.

How many tears can one
shed in a day?

I keep looking for answers
afraid I will get lost in
all the noise.

Today

You were not able to give me
    when I was young
    when you were young
what you can give me today.

You were not able to be there for me
    when I was young
    when you were young
like you were there for me today.

You were not able to do for me
    when I was young
    when you were young
what you've done for me today.

You were not able to be
    when I was young
    when you were young
who you are to me today.

And that's okay.

Because you are who you are
  you do for me, give to me
    care for me and love me
all that you could not
    when I was young

when you were young

when we knew less
than we knew today.

HSP

I can feel itchy scratching
like someone poking me
with a sharp point toothpick
at the base of my neck.
I shudder,
swat at the offender,
a clothing label tag.
A swollen gland
that would have anyone else
just achy,
sends me into massive
illness overtime.
All symptoms possible
displayed extreme.
I cannot believe
this is what a simple
cold does to me.
The tapping of a finger,
the ticking of a clock,
upside down pan shots
on the TV
all of these and so
much more.
Little things
do such drastic things
to me.

Expression

Expression, we think of as
  music, art, novels or
            pictures.
Concrete products
  to see, touch, feel, read,
            absorb.
But expression is everyday
  every thought
    every second of everyday
            is expression.
Thoughts just don't go
            away
they find friends to
  come along and
    come back to you singing
the song that you
      taught it
          to sing.

Serendipity

Serendipity
is a friend of mine.
I picture her with long
voluptuous hair and a
silken dress blowing
in her essence.

But
I've never actually seen
serendipity.

Serendipity's a little like
God.

She gives me clues along
the journey of life
to show me which ways
are wrong and are right
for me
and I believe
she loves me.

But, God to me is an
ominous idea,
plagued with old rituals,
incense and rules,
that never made any rational sense.

God is boxed
and rigid,
rarely allowing room
for growth.

Old school
for good 'ol boys
and reborn convicts,
for grandmothers who never
questioned existence,
teenagers looking for friends
and parents looking to
control children.

As much power as people
give the word God
it really is a small one to me.

Serendipity
on the other hand
rolls on the tongue
ends with an up note
and a sometimes vowel
swirl.

Serendipity
much more fits me,
free spirit, artist, seeker.

Nothing in our plane of
understanding
can prove much more to us
about life than cause and effect.

And if taken objectively,
without the fear, guilt and shame
associated with "god"
we can see the pattern.

Perhaps we are not just
spectators in life
after all.

Toddler Inspiration

"Mommy, where do dreams live?"
she asked with innocent eyes.
Her mother shocked, surprised
at the question coming
from her two year old child
replied,
"Well, I guess
dreams live up in the sky.
Our minds go there when
we lay down to rest
to a place of wonder
and peacefulness.
That's where dreams live I guess."
Her daughter
satisfied with the reply
went back to counting numbers
and naming shapes
but left her mother with
a puzzled look upon her face.
Where do dreams live?
She thought to herself.
What do kids know
that we do not?

Soul Lovers

Looking back upon my life as I enter
this new journey, faces, places,
feelings whelming up inside.
How I came to be here, all the
changes, the moves, the searching, the
poems, incorporated into who I am now.
Acceptance of this whole self
is recent.
Reality of hidden dreams imminent.
Chapters upon chapters marking
layers to my soul.
And here I am
faced with a new challenge, a change
to experience more than all I've seen
combined, a chance to share those
revelations with another, to learn, to
grow, to achieve a paradise for life.
You surprised me, more so
someone, something surprised us.
Able to see behind the outer coverings
we have become the closest of friends,
the greatest of lovers. Five weeks combined
full of a lifetime of memories, a library
of books.
My vision of the future expanded with one
look in your eyes, cut from the same
crystal. Grateful for each day, each second

for this path. I reflect on all those
        that brought me here.
How ironic to find you have
        been there the whole time,
    sporadically placed in dreams, desires, four
lined poems dashed in a minute of future
        recollection. This is not of our control.
This is not of our creation. This
        is a gift from one who loves us and knows
us best. An answer to the prayer of
a seven year old unaware her prince lived
        down the street tormented by his own
demons.
So similar our lives have been,
        so different we arrived at the same
conclusions
    at the same time, in the same dimension and
I who have shed the need of other's god believe
        in a force more powerful, described in
    only visions. For a love this strong
can only be the result of magic.

Life is a Dance

Life is a dance
  meant to be shared.
By partner's entwined
  in each other's arms.

Sunset and sunrise
  together hand in hand.
Sometimes one taking
  the lead.
Sometimes one flying
  the other catching.

Always helping each other
  up after a fall.

Risk taking, adventure seeking
  the dance continues.

Souls sweeping across
  the dance of life.

Love the choreographer.

The Adventure

Something is coming
        the signs say it so.
Only 100 more miles
        to the Nirvana road.
I can only get there
        if I keep my car in gear.
But people on the side
        of the road
Call "Come, come help me dear."

And a banjo player
        sing to me throwing
  diamonds and rubies and song.
Sweet tender neediness
  with that you can't
        go wrong.

But the sign says
  Only 100 miles to go.
And I need to get there
        don't you know?
Something waiting
        bigger than all this,
  I'll send you a postcard.

Read Me

I read the words of other's yesterday
I'd never read before.
So alike in form and nature
  I understand their core.
Words I'd heard from other source
  echoing through time.
They know.
Someone knows.
A world, I have just touched the tip.
A vision unreal. Beings like me!
I found you. How surprised I should be
  to find them too. Magic.
Yet, the concept of this life surprised me.
The course I am on, a path unto my dreams
  frightens me.
I am but a child
  in a place
I've been known as a Master.
Commonality. Competition.
May I learn from you.
May you one day
  read me.

Moments

There are moments
so powerful you can
almost step out of body
and see.
This is it. This is one
of those moments.

Birth. Death. Life. These
are moments.
Marriage. First steps
and last illnesses. Moments.

But so are too those
heart to heart conversations
when all the walls come
down and raw realness
is presented in a word, a comment,
a tear.

Memorable moments.
Life altering moments.

Moments even memory
cannot capture completely.
Yet, time never
forgets.

Air

It's cold rain that fell on me as I ran
  to put out the last bag of trash on the curb.
But, the cold rain had a smell as fresh as fresh
  can be and this cold rain
as it fell, it washed me and my garbage clean.

That's what outside air does for me.
As though all the trash I hold
  in my heart, in my body, my mind
while locked in four wall capacity,
it all flies away when freed to the air
  clearing my mind, my soul
all I am and all I hope to be.

I need fresh air more than love.

It is my element,
  my sense of natural oneness
with the universe.
Washing me clean,
on a cold, calm, beautiful
  rainy night.

Dragonfly Dance

I never watched a dragonfly dance
until today.
Down by the pond, over flown
with half a dozen inches
of torrent rain from yesterday,
the dragonfly dances
the dance of love.
Fluttering one way
stop
reverse
turn
and off straight again.
Above the muddy water they skim.
Reflection of sunlight,
making love mid flight.
Oh, to be a dragonfly.
Power of dual wing beats.
The need for water, air, love.
I'd fly, dream and die
Dancing with the Dragonfly.

The Frog and the Fly, a Story

Once upon a time
there sat a tree frog
on a leaf
sitting as frogs do
croaking a bit
crooked at times,
but vocalizing nonetheless
when a fly came by to
say hello,
a nice sort of chap
with an English accent.
The frog,
perhaps because he was
a bit crooked,
did not leap out his tongue
and munch the small fry
down.
But instead asked him over
for tea,
as a good British fellow would do
and they had
a very nice
conversation.
Not the sort about money
or politics or god forbid
religion!
Heavens! No!

No, they spoke of allegories,
metaphors and how
perhaps
the fact that the fly said
'hello'
and the frog did not eat him,
but crumpets instead,
perhaps that may have
just a little bit
changed the evolution
of the world.
For the crumpets were delicious
and the tea just right
and afterwards they
took a long nap.
During which time they both went
back to being a fly and a frog.
Gulp! Good-Night.

In Comparison

I read
of artists nesting,
decorating, doing what they love,
making space their own.

I see
artists workshops,
created specially, individually
a reflection of self.

But,
instead of inspiration,
sensation, of my own artistic
self,
I feel weak in comparison.

I read
books of knowledge, mysteries
and novels,
filled with the wisdom of life.

I see
authors on TV
promoting their work,
getting praised, getting paid,
an acceptance of self.
But instead of insight,

delight, pride at what they
have done,
I feel pressured to be
something I'm not.

And I know
the sadness from the realization
that I cannot find joy
in others success
because I feel incomplete
in my own,
encompasses my soul.

But it lets me know,
I have much
to learn

from them.

Easy Way Out

Life is difficult.
There is a 0% survival rate
and the in-between
fraught with memories
buried
deep in psychosis
and
long lost reasons why.
We fight to retain sanity.
Putting priority on
necessary items
everyday living.
Fighting the
now.
Living for
tomorrow.
Driven by demons of
yesterday.
We cannot hide.
And the belief that others have lives
easier than our own
is only to mask the fear
that
this is all there is.
And if there isn't
anything more
anything less

then
nothing compares.
We are set upon
a universal individual adventure.
Circumstances unknown
to the babe we once were.
Life creates its own illusion and
the fight of life
or purpose if you will
is to shed the patterns
of others
and to create your own.
To name. To claim.
Your own personal outlook on life.
To justify
the difficulty of living.
But there is
No Easy Way Out.

Memories Left in a Tan

The sweet smell of a cool breeze
  rides on the air tonight.
As crickets chirp a melody
  words cannot describe.
The sun sinking lower
  earlier every day
makes me know that summer's
  going, going, gone,
leaving memories along the way.
Memories of a day at the
  beach with four young friends.
Memories of flowers blossoms
  all colors and all hues, shapes, sizes
and scents.
Memories of hot, hot sun
  melting on skin,
the afterglow of a heat filled day.
Memories left in a tan.
Memories grilling late
  when the sunset doesn't start until 10pm
and firecrackers that rang through the night
welcomed summer in.
Memories of a season come
  and a season leaving too soon.
Memories to be held close to
  the heart when the snow flies
once again.

I Wished I Believed in a god

I wished I believed in a god
like other people do, go to
church on Sunday, kneel
in the pews and know
there are answers.

I wished I believed in a job
as a means to get ahead,
go to work, come home,
get up, go to bed.
Basic.

I wished I believed in a home
as where one's heart does lie,
what we can afford will have
to do, the neighbors are funny,
but we're saving money,
look how wise we are.

I wished I believed in a love,
simple, faithful and true,
and if you love him enough,
you can surely make up
love enough for two.

Everyday lives.
Everyday people.

Common bonds.
Common needs.
Common wants.

Satisfied with what there is
or isn't quite enough.

How easy life would be. But me?
No. I can't let sleeping dogs lie.
I question, scrutinize, dream
and ask Why?

I wished I believed in a god
that sent down rays from above,
to hold and protect me, love
and shelter me in this world
and the next.

But life for me has never
been that simple.

The Walls Between Us

We really never touch anything.
Science has proven
   electrons negatively react to
one another
   and push away instinctively.

We never really touch anything.
Or so the story goes.
Energy between, among us.
We have more space
   within us than black holes.

We never really touch memories.
Yet, they are as real as today.
And feelings?
Feelings are merely
   chemical reactions.
Appear colorful on a screen
      but really do not mean anything
to the one crying.

We never really touch
      or so it would seem.
But, if we never really
  experience any of this. Could it be?
This is all
      but a dream?

Dreams

New day has begun.
I've tried to run and run
but I've only ended up here.
So accomplished so it seems
then why do I only dream
my whole life waiting for me
on a shelf too high
for me to reach.

Words

She reached for the Bic I held in my hand
  and began to write on the wall.
That two year old child did things different
  never got into dolls or balls.

At six months she began exploring without
  the protection of Mom.
Protection she provided herself
  without using a fist or a palm.
That blood curdling scream works as well
  now as it did then, excellent protection against
all sorts of men.

But she had a passion for life, yes she did.
From place to place she'd run.
As she grew older
  the places grew further apart.
When she moved away it broke my heart.

But she grew up and grew out of the places
  she went.
Eventually came back home,
  only to find the security she sought had been
here all along.

But, off running she went again 'til she
  came to the edge of the world.

Lines of blue water waves unfurled
  toes curled in the sand.

She longed to leave dry land,
  so off she went again.
Racing boats
  took her far into waters deep, but when she
saw the down dark depths, did she run?
No, she leaped!

She took off swimming laps around,
  the fishes were her friends.
Until one day the north wind blew
  and put her fun to an end.
But she stayed at the edge of that pool,
  the big puddle by her home and
stared up at the sky and began to
  dream of how to fly.

My, oh my, she'll never stop,
  off again she goes.
So if you see her, listen close
  and she'll her tale of how at birth
she came out kicking and its
  life worth living
she puts first.

But more than likely, she will fly away,

  leaving behind only signs
of a Bic pen and words, words, words,
telling you where she's been.

Nighttime Lifetime

The day is over
but my work
has just begun.
I will fill
the hours
so many seem to think
as rest, with
fighting prowess to the
test.
I will battle.
I will struggle.
I will win.
I will lose.
I will experience.
I will feel.
I will learn.
I will explore.
I will remember.
I will know.

And you just call it
sleep.

In Honor

I want you to know
you are beautiful
just as you are.

Your hair in rollers
covered in pink swath
matching your clean mauve shirt
folded hands.

I want you to know
you are wonderful
just as you are.

No coffee to tend.
No sewing to mend.
No dinner to put leftovers away.

You are simply wonderful.
Just being you.

I want you to know
we love you
just as you are.

Your smile, now crooked
still warms my heart
as you make me laugh

with your straight shooting
sense of humor style.

Your wit has never skipped a beat
although you now must sleep and sleep.

We still love you
just as you are.

You never had to do anything
to make us love you.
No bread too delicious to pass up.
No spread on the table too thin.
No strict tough love that hid
the gentle soul
the quiet strength within.

Those were the icing on the cake
that is you.

And now that you have reached
a part of life
that won't let you do, do, do.
Do you realize
we still love you?

We love you for the you
you are.

Not the you
you used to be.

We love you for what you offer now.

If only a sight for us to see
a woman braving her toughest years
with might and dignity.

Do you know? Do you feel?
Do you see?

We love you for you.

All that you did.
All that you do.

Was always icing to me.

The Lacey Legacy

A tear fell slowly down my check tonight
as I lay wondering what the future holds
for this tiny life of mine.
And I missed a woman I knew
for such a short time
but whose passion, purity, vitality rivaled mine
ancestral passings through time.
It was if she were holding
the babe I once was
in her soft aged hands.
As I lay quiet, I remembered her strength
I knew instinctively as a child.
And memories, I know,
are clouded with love
but love is what keeps her alive.
And I thought to myself,
what will they think of me?
Once I've vanished into thin air?
The one love that I leave to this world
for the ones that may might remember me
is this
words upon words upon words upon words
in books bound by round metal loops.
A poetry of life I create and will make
that shall be my legacy.

You Just Know

You told me you just knew
and I knew that you did.
Because sometimes in life
you just know what you know.
And you can't explain
how or why
but you knew when
instantly.
The best things in life
are not planned.
They are created.
Not by you or I
but by fate or destiny.
Pure chemistry.
The birth of a star.
We like to say
we know it all
to take it
nice and slow.
But we know so little
how this universe really works.
You just know when you know.
And I'm glad
you did.

Mother Earth

My lady in the lake
she sang to me today.
Dancing beneath the rippled waves
spirals of spun light
sparkled pure harmonic symphony.
I saw what she needed me to see
the cobwebs of society cleaned free.
She revealed to me a purpose, a goal
a world of fairytale dreams.
I gave myself to her
while Cliff Swallows dived in her breeze.
So hard my life has seemed
but she has been there
each step along the way.
She has been my savior
my queen.
Without hesitation
I dedicate my life
to the beauty of the day
the guiding moon at night and
the shimmering of the lake.
Her song my beacon of light
guiding me home.

Remember

I had forgotten
  about the great wings
of the Blue Heron
 in flight
as it landed before
   me in the park
        today.

I had forgotten about
   the baby muskrat
that all the kids
   said looked like
 a beaver from far away.

I had forgotten about
   the flash of orange
as an oriole flew
   over my head. The
peeking red of
   the sun as the clouds
melted the sunset
   and the pale full moon
 rising.

I had forgotten
   all of that
as soon as my feet came

inside. Television on.
Laundry to finish and
keep me busy.

Until tired I sat down
and it hit me.
I had forgotten
about all
I promised myself
I would not forget.

Musings

I sat in the
early evening
light of day
next to a woman
who shares my DNA

and listened to stories
of long ago yesterday
and what may come
up in the garden
next year

when hopefully we will
come and sit here
together again
to admire the
Cosmos grow.

House of Love

I can hear your children
running around, playing the
piano, stomping on the ground.
A chaotic house of love.
I can see your husband
The Look on his face
wanting you to get off the phone
as he drags another bag of
laundry to the table.
I can see your reluctance
in letting go.
But you are needed and
I was happy just to
hear your voice.
It is a luxury quite often
taken for granted.
Friends who give us perspective.
I can smell the
scented candle burning,
food cooking in the kitchen.
All my senses reunited
across wires of telephone line
strung from pole to pole to pole.
I can be, if only for a moment,
in your house of love.

Speculation

If I am alone on the beach
I feel free.
Let go.
Smile, arms outstretched
toward
the sky
hugging the vastness.
I let go. Lose me.
Become one with all I see.
I lose them.
Find me in
one glorious moment.
An incredible feeling
of love
and understanding.

But the moment a person
shows up
walking dog down the
same sand path
I chose to follow.
I warp back into
the skin I'm in.
Zap back to ego mode
walls-up, guarded
protecting the spirit
that let go such a

short time ago.
Only humans do this to me.
Put me on edge
feel as though I'm
being watched, judged.

Hawks let me soar.
Red birds celebrate me.
With nature I am free.

But humans.
Humans disconnect,
intersect, evaluate, intellectuate,
devour spirit with egomaniac
competitive attraction.

Maybe that is why we are
so awful
to each other.
Why we wall in
who we really are.
Always a display.
Always on stage.

Maybe we all need
more time alone
with the waves.

Talking about Death and Dying

She talked of a friend dying
  and words not said
when given the chance
        to say them.

She talked of fear
when
no one talks.
no one learns.
no one listens.

Life can be as lonely as
  death appears to be.

She talked about death,
  I thought about life
and how now is
  always the time to talk
        about dying.

For to live with death
    as a friend
not enemy
    makes
  it a natural part
        of life.
We fear loss of self

but if you have shown the
world love and felt it in return
you know immortality.

And you accept the
lives
that
live
on.

Beautiful

I am here and it is beautiful!

More beautiful than you
could ever imagine
and the clouds florescent green
just because I wished them so!

I am here and I am fine.

The life that lived, although I
called it mine, one part of a
miraculous journey that
never begins nor ends.

So hard to understand there
so easy to see now.

If everyone could see how
beautiful it is, they'd join me!
But you are there, crying,
wondering where I am.
I am here. I am fine and
it
is beautiful!

Trendy

Friends are like sweaters.
Some are worn all year round just
because of their softness and durability.

Some last a season.

Some are put on the shelf,
tag still on, until they are donated
the next summer
to someone who would appreciate them more.

Some look good in the store
but when you get them on at home
they just don't fit right.

Some work with all outfits.

Some only with jeans, riding horses.

And some are such high maintenance,
dry clean only permanent press
that it takes too much work
to keep them around very long.

Either and all ways
friends, like sweaters, are a
critical part of any outfit.

And I, for one, am grateful for
the style my friends add
to the fabric of my life.

For My Mother

When I am thinking hard
  or worried or stressed
or sometimes just even bored
I tap my fingers
  thumb to tip, each one
over and over again.
  Just like you.

When I laugh out loud
  at something surprisingly funny
ironic or plain truth.
I throw my head back,
  eyes sealed shut
mouth a beautiful smile
  and a low rumble laugh
comes out, sounding
  just like you.

When I sing

even a single note
you are there.

My voice is yours,
so identical on the phone
family would mistake us.

I need my morning caffeine,
my nightly awakenings
and hours upon hours
to fully function normally
when I am up before others' morning
just like you.

I love the water
as you do.
Breaststroke please,
water in my eyes stings.
I'd wear glasses if I didn't
have contacts, ah,

sunglasses will do.

I cry like you,
  how upsetting to be sad
and hear your voice
    crying with me
coming out of my own mouth!

Good thing I smile like
  you too.

So much of who I am
  everyday.
My need to write.
My love of news.
My capacity to read
  really, really fast
and still comprehend.

My spitfire stubbornness

in arguments about
life, issues, politics and principles.
All learned from you.

My love of the universe
all things wondrous
stars that fall
flowers that bloom
and even rainy days too.
All learned from you!

I carry with me your gene
of depression
sadness that seeps into my
bones.

But, so too, do I carry with
me that can do strength
passed on a generation
or two.

You've taught me perseverance
to keep moving on.
No matter what life
throws at me.

You've taught me how to be
strong,
and gentle and kind and sweet
at the same time tough
enough to be on my own
in any kind of street.

All I wish for you is happiness
as I'm sure you wish me too.

But today, today of all your days,
I simply want you to know
how very proud I am
to be so very much
like you.

Wonder

In the Spirit of Sophia

I sat in the sun reading
 a book on Angels
I walked on the beach
 talking to the sky
I held a child and gave
 her healing
I watched a fire while
 listening to its wisdom
I bathed in moonlight
 rippling down
I filled my chalice
 with spiritual surrender
And I
 became One

Creativity

What thoughts what feelings
    have you thought I
            to be able to express in art
    visual form of beauty.
You possess talent I could
        never learn.
Admiration mutual as you read
    my journal of life.
I take no credit
    nor you do yours.
Gifts of expression
      are not to be boasted.
For there is a connection
    with something beyond our reach
          that flies through fingertips
into thought and form.
No message do we hear
      or calling from above.
Just a steady rhythm
    through our hearts
    through our lungs.
The muse she then takes over
    as any artist knows.
Though painter or writer,
    musician or preacher.
      It is not I creating thus.
It is what one cannot explain

as though the pieces
finally fit.
A fairy named Tink is an
answer to some.
But I feel the pounding
the rhythm of the drum
as a pulsating energy
a vibration, a sound.
We as a planet on a tiny cell
in a newborn child.
This is what creates expression.

ABC

I do not need FACTS
 to prove.
This is right.
This is wrong.

I do not need ABSOLUTES
 to see.
He is weak.
I am strong.

I do not need PROVEN THEORIES
 to know.
Who I am.
Who I'm not.

I do not need SCIENTIST or POLITICIANS
 to legislate my life.

For life is fluid. Change is constant.
And boxing in answers
 makes the questions violent.

And when we try to put life in a
 nice, neat package
Fed-Ex style
 it only leaks out like chocolate ice
cream on a Texas

highway
melting deliciously down
the seams.

Life cannot be contained.
Answers cannot be boxed.
That is why there will always
be room for
artists and poets
philosophers and writers
musicians and lyricists.

For truth lies not
in the books
but in the beholders.

Kali

What my heart longs to feel
    is a soul like yours against mine.
Energy forces colliding
    we would tumble any wall.
Passion the fuel to our
    burning desire.
Each day would be an adventure.
In gender I find the parts
    not discriminatory.
A body only houses a spirit.
I dream of connection
    body, mind and soul.
Each person a prospect
    under rigorous strain
to be all I need them to be.
I exist beyond the realm of reality
    as only few people do.
So close to the truth
    I cause fear.
So far from expectation
    I invade lives.
I cannot compromise
    my first mistake.
A broken heart takes long to heal.
And imagination goes awry
    with one kiss, one smile,
I am living alternate realities.

It is not on the fault of those
    I choose as prey.
But on my own shoulders do I rest
    the pain of expectation.
Deny me not, I pray,
    to each to pass my way.
But on and on I go
    traveling this road alone.

Moths in the Moonlight

I fight what I am
what I do
every second of every day.
I forgot I am not like others
and seemingly displace
the responsibility given to me.
To record.
A scribe among the masses.
I see so much more.
It walls up inside me
like screams in a dream
that won't make any sound.
It eats me alive.
Dries up my blood.
Tears my eyes
and laughs.
It is the only drug
capable of cure.
And the peace does come
like the rush of a pipe
a landing safely
from a roller coaster ride.
Filling my soul from the
inside out.
Moths in the moonlight
my release.

A Year Since

We flew last night
in a '52 Studebaker
  spiffed up boat of a car.

Flew right over traffic
   you and I.
We did loop-de-loops
  upside down over the bridge
   where people were lined
up in their tiny cars
  locked in traffic, earth bound.

We raced, hit 95, 100 mph
  yet I felt no fear.
Top down, upside down.
I held onto the roll bar
  to keep from falling out
while you drove, flying.
Yet, still. No fear.

You drove me to a relative's house
  still here.

And left me to go check on the car,
not trusting neighbors to cherish your
  prized possession as you did.
I continued on in my dream,

and you continued on in yours.

But, we both knew we had
just taken the trip of many
  lifetimes
flying high in the night sky.

No words needed.
Nothing conceded.
Simply time, spent flying
  you and I together.

Finally I could trust you
  to drive.

Morning Glories

Morning Glories growing
in cement entwined.
Growing, growing, glowing
like the creations in my mind.
They should grow
on the trellis
it took me three hours to assemble.
They should grow in the garden
next to the sunflower fellows.
But Morning Glories grow
wherever it is they wish.
Freedom found at my fingertips
and a dream that showed me
to believe
I have to accept
sometimes
Morning Glories grow
underneath
cement.

Problems

I have a problem. Just one. But, this problem puts all other problems to shame. I have an overactive imagination.

I worry, a product of my problem. But not normal, everyday I hope I get to work on time worry. No, I worry about the end of the world and the fate of the species.

I worry I've gained a pound and the crumbling of nations. Oh! Don't get me started. Imagine living without money or food or necessities and having no power to get any. I worry about that.

But, my problems are more than global. I mean worry is useless, right? So I begin to fear. I begin to fear loneliness, rejection, regret. I begin to fear failure, love and others' respect. I begin to exaggerate moments trivial to the scene. I take them, expand them as if in a dream.

My fear then turns to self-pity, and Oh! What I do with that. The illogic a female mind can create, insecurity at its best.

Of course, my problem isn't always a problem. It goes much deeper than that. My problem creates fantasy worlds from a garden as big as a hat. Fairies are real to me. Birds talk and I to them. Flowers, you know, are the best kind of friends.

And the water! Oh, my problem lets her create on her own. (She does a much better job than I.)

Both sides of the coin, my problem erupts, emphasizing good and bad. So, if my problem's so even, you ask as I say, What's the matter with that?

Nothing. Nothing at all, if it were blended together as one. A good thought, a bad and back to good again would make me a happy lass.

No. My problem's a problem because, you see, my problem has control of me. A perfectly fine day flittered with fluffy clouds can turn ominous with one frown, one scowl.

And then the problem sets to work, rolling and rolling, I wonder, what if, poor me. Until all my fears come true.

How do I stop it? If I knew, I wouldn't be talking to you!

You for You

I left with feelings of regret.
I didn't know how you would make it
without me.
I didn't know if you would
forget me.
I didn't realize how much I
affected you.
So I come back now and then to
see you
and I am so proud you are
making it on your own.
I am so proud that you finally
took my advice
and threw your heart into the
life you have chosen.
But more than that
it warms my heart to see
my things, my projects
are still a part of your life.
I am happy for you
and that makes me love you
more than I ever thought
I could.
Because you are happy without me.
You have found your own place
in this world.
You have found your own courage

your own strength.
And that feeds my soul
more than any need
I have to be needed.
So I leave you again.
This time a little calmer
more peaceful
because I know I am still
a part of you
and the wonderful person
you have become.

Contagious

It is said that as
one forms a smile
the brain perceives
happiness
no matter what mood the
person making the smile
happens to be in.
My theory is that once the smile
is in place, it only takes
another person near smiling
to create a giggle
and then laughter
and then love.

Calling

I followed the sun today
peeking out
from a patch
of blue sky
on the horizon.

It called to me
like my dreams of
what could be
shining off so far away,
I can see it.
But the further and further
I drove,
the farther and farther
it flew

until I almost ran
out of gas
gave up, turned around
and went back
to the place I live
closed in, no view.

But the sun was too inviting
and the colors on the
trees started to flow
and the air smelled

sweeter and the
wind became calmer

and I knew I had
to keep driving on.

So I followed the dream
of blue sky sunshine
as far as I could go
to where land meets the sea
meets the sky meets

me.

Smile Strain

It's the light shine
in your eyes
reflected.
And the way that
you smile at me.
It's your arms
around me tight.
Your kisses good-night.
The daylight hours
spent together.
And now I leave
you after so much
time spent grinning,
I remember your eyes
and the sound
of your laughter.

Knowing You

You can't control me
anymore
with your questions
your insults
your shots
made in the name of concern
of love.

You can't scare me
anymore
with your sucking eyes
that bore into my weakness.
Prey on me vampire style
until I turn zombie and
believe your lies.

You can't berate me
beat me into submission
verbally
until I admit you are right
I am wrong
always wrong.

You can't make me question
myself
my life
my existence

because I know now
why I am here.

I know my purpose.

I have my plans
for my life.
I do not need your approval
or your permission
to be me.

I do not need you to tell
me who I am.
Who I should be.
What I should do.
Wear. Eat. Sleep.

You cannot manipulate me
any longer.
I am not your slave
your servant
your puppet.
I am me.
And I know myself so well
you cannot tell me who I am
any longer.

You cannot control me.

But you try.
You will always try.

At least until
you find you
and discover the power
you so desperately seek
over me
cannot come from controlling others.

It can only come from
knowing.
you.

Acceptance

Knock it up to experience.
A night lived with good intentions
the been there done that girl.
You may succeed in one area
and the praise you receive
is far greater
than my satisfaction in where
I have been.
Although different.
We are both mind and soul
obsessed with success
admiration, trust.
Different, yet equal
we share
A common interest in I.
So I wipe away the tears
of what could've been.
And look at my life
through the perspective
of who I am, what I've seen,
what I've learn and done
and walk away
Proud of who I've become.

One Tear Drop

It isn't your sassy-fras pants
that make me love you so
or that opinionated
"I told you so" you love
to tell so well.

It isn't the way you toss
your hair
when you think that no one's
looking,
or that wiggle you give
when you smile thinking
about your kids.

No.

It's because out of all you
have been through
all you are and all you've done
you are just you
perfectly, perfectly you.

You make no excuses,
apologies or lies,
feel no need to go lay down
and cry.
You just live in the moment

react when hurt
punch when tested

and stand up for yourself
and your own needs.

There's no games, no fussing,
no playing, no mussing.
Just wonderful, beautiful,
smart, sassy, sweet, booty kicking
you.

And at the end of the day
that's enough
for me.

Raccoon Memories

I scared the raccoon again
as I stepped out into
the thick snow
opening the sliding glass doors
onto the moonlit patio
where the raccoon
had been, once again,
trying to eat the birdseed
his huge belly over slung
the round squirrel guard,
his legs beneath the bottom
his arms reaching the top
where like treasure lay
all those sunflower seeds
for the taking.
He reminded me
of masks and night
of stealing those sweet moments
when you think no one
is watching
to snack on riches that lie
under the moonlight.

The Art of Writing

I tried to draw my sophomore year
in high school.
A bear, a block, a bunch of fruit
ended up looking like muck.
I kept at it for awhile,
I'd never say die at once.
But the feeling never came.
No satisfaction did I find
in teddy bears
or what my pencil had drawn.
So I quit.
Why waste time on the inevitable.
I began to sculpt, to craft, to sew,
I even painted a little.
But never did I draw.
Yet sitting here, describing life
with pen on paper clean,
I realized,
I can draw! I am an artist
after all.

Ordinary? Never.

Sometimes the wonder of
 the minute miracles of our
  ordinary life

like watching a child grow or
snow form, fall, melt and flow
away into a river that turns to rain
that makes a seed turn to a stem that
births a flower
that feeds a bee
that

stops me dead in my tracks.

Zen Madness

I can talk existence
existentialism, environmental myths
and rhythms.
I can talk quarks and biotechnologies,
quantum happenings and
theories beyond questioned
understanding.
I can talk.
But to live?
To live
I still must put one foot in front of
another.
I still must decide
what to eat. wear. do.
each day.
Clothing is not optional
in society or winter.
I am a philosopher
of the greatest poetic sort.
But I must still
pay bills
and keep in contact
with relatives
I claim
to know.
Life is consistent in
its neediness.

And this
neediness is consistent
in bringing me down
from the heavens
to earth. to ground. to life. to me.
merely human.
Chopping wood. carry water.
Life goes on.

The Hamster in my Head

There is a hamster that lives
inside my head
he runs around at all
hours.

Wakes me in the middle of dreams
forcing me to run barefoot
fast, half blind down
steep stairs
to grab pen and paper.

I do not know if he
ever sleeps.
I wonder if he stops to eat.
I know he makes me so,
donuts, chocolate, soda pop.
He does love his sweets
they speed him, go.

I picture him in his wheel
up there
high on sugared pie
running and running
his little tongue hanging out
sweatband on his head
shoes on his feet.
Is he listening to Eye of the Tiger?

I wonder so
for he does believe he is
the champion.

He does not see how
his speeding around
drives me crazy
to tears
even stops me in the middle of life
to record that which
he churns out.
For most of what you see
here today
is due in part to him.

Somewhere on that little
ticker taped filled litter
lies a word or two
VISIONS.
And today here we are
catching up to him.

I'd like to write him a
lullaby
perhaps that's why he likes
calm music
or the waves at night
when everyone's asleep

and all you can hear
is the sound of the moon
calling.

I am grateful to thee
the Hamster in my Head.

But, would you slow down
please?

It's time for me to bed.
There will be enough time
for more running
in the morning.

To find our more about Jeannine Proulx,
her poetry, her life, her passion,
please visit her website
at
www.jeannineproulx.com

Other books by Jeannine Proulx

WORD PLAY

The Ne-Ne News Book

Spilled Ink
(a Holland Writer's Workshop Collaboration)

Books available for purchase on
Amazon.com
or
www.jeannineproulx.com

Here's to the visions to come!